Gloria Eveleigh

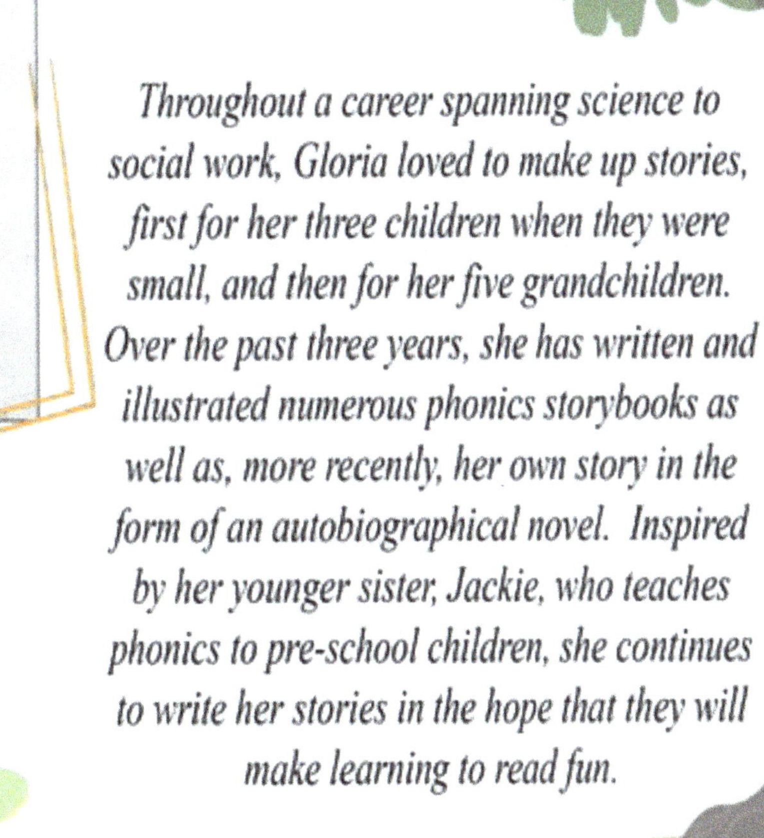

Throughout a career spanning science to social work, Gloria loved to make up stories, first for her three children when they were small, and then for her five grandchildren. Over the past three years, she has written and illustrated numerous phonics storybooks as well as, more recently, her own story in the form of an autobiographical novel. Inspired by her younger sister, Jackie, who teaches phonics to pre-school children, she continues to write her stories in the hope that they will make learning to read fun.

Titan the Time- Travelling Tiger

By Gloria Eveleigh

The /t/ sound is emboldened throughout this story to enable the reader to recognise and practice it.

Titan is a magnificent tiger.
Titan lives in a country called Tibet.

Other tigers think that titan is terrific because

he can travel through time.

Titan touches his toes, twitches his tail, and

' TADDAH'

He can revisit any part of his long life.
Titan is not sure in which part of his life he is

happiest.

Sometimes Titan feels tender hearted.
He touches his toes, twitches his tail, and

'TADDAH!'

He travels back to when he is a teeny tiny
tiger.
Timid and trusting little Titan tries to
play.

His mummy tiger takes care of him

As Titan gets bigger, his daddy tiger tus-
sles andtumbles with him.

Sometimes Daddy tickles Titan.
Sometimes he tosses Titan into the air.

Titan and his daddy have a tremendous
time together

Together, Mummy and Daddy Tiger tenderly tuck Titan up for the night.

Sometimes Titan feels wild.
He touches his toes, twitches his tail, and

'TADDAH'...

He travels back to when he is teenage tiger.
Titan, the teenage tiger is tetchy and easily
upset.

His parents have to 'tread carefully' to
avoid

Titan having a temper tantrum.

Titan torments the girl tigers for fun. He finds a girlfriend called Tammy who thinks

Titan is trendy.

Titan loves Tammy in her lovely twinkly pink tutu.

Sometimes Titan feels tired.
He touches his toes, twitches his tail, and

'TADDAH!'...

He travels forward to when he is very old tiger.
The old Titan tans himself in the sun while he
drinks his favourite tipple.

The old, sun-tanned Titan has lots of time
to teach the tiny tigers.

He is tender and tolerant, and tells them
exciting tales.

However, Titan is the toast of all the other tigers in Tibet the way he is right now. He is handsome, toned and very strong.

So even though Titan can time-travel, he now knows he is happiest living in the present.

THE END